My Life as a

JEW

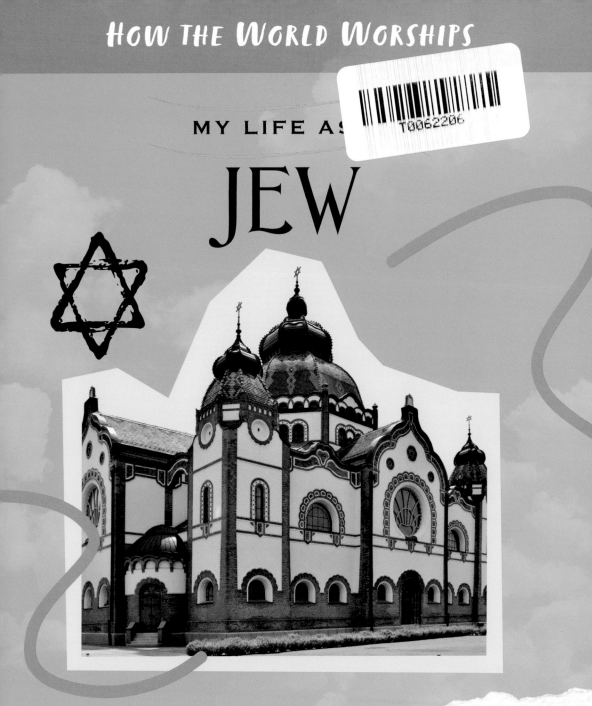

Jennifer Kleiman

REVISED EDITION

T0062206

45TH PARALLEL PRESS

Published in the United States of America by Cherry Lake Publishing Group
Ann Arbor, Michigan
www.cherrylakepublishing.com

Editorial Consultant: Dr. Virginia Loh-Hagan, EdD, Literacy, San Diego State University
Reading Adviser: Beth Walker Gambro, MS, Ed., Reading Consultant, Yorkville, IL

Photo Credits: © Snezana Vasiljevic/Shutterstock, cover, 1; © Petr Pohudka/Shutterstock, 4; © Pavel Kusmartsev/
Dreamstime.com, 7; © LaraP_photo/Shutterstock, 10; © Monkey Business Images/Dreamstime.com, 13;
© Donna Ellen Coleman/Shutterstock, 14; © yhelfman/Shutterstock, 16; © Michael Siluk/Shutterstock, 17;
© Angelo Gilardelli/Dreamstime.com, 18; © TalyaAL/Shutterstock, 19; © Sopotnicki/Shutterstock, 20;
© Derek Brumby/Shutterstock, 21; © Katerinalin/Dreamstime.com, 24; © Perachel paz Mark/Shutterstock, 26;
© Jim West/Alamy Stock Photo, 28; © Chayim Ehrenfeld/Shutterstock, 29; © Sergii Koval/Shutterstock, 30

Copyright © 2024 by Cherry Lake Publishing Group
All rights reserved. No part of this book may be reproduced or utilized in any form or by any means
without written permission from the publisher.

45th Parallel Press is an imprint of Cherry Lake Publishing Group.

Library of Congress Cataloging-in-Publication Data has been filed and is available at catalog.loc.gov.

Printed in the United States of America
Corporate Graphics

AUTHOR'S NOTE:

My Life as a Jew is written for a general audience. It is meant to share with its readers a few fundamental beliefs and traditions of the Jewish faith, a bit of history, and a glimpse into the rich tapestry of Jewish life around the globe. While the lives in this book may differ from yours, they are based on the authentic experiences of real Jews living in the United States and Israel.

TABLE OF CONTENTS

Did you know? Jewish customs and beliefs are not all the same. They can be very different. There are different denominations, or groups of beliefs and practices. People also practice Judaism differently in different places. The roots of the faith keep the whole tree strong.

INTRODUCTION

Religions are systems of faith and worship. Do you practice a religion? About 80 percent of the world's population does. That's 4 out of 5 people. Every religion is different. Some have one God. That's called **monotheism**. Other religions have multiple gods. This is called polytheism. Some religions have an **icon** instead of a god. An icon is an important figure.

Judaism is the world's oldest monotheistic religion still practiced today. Two other major monotheistic religions are Christianity and Islam. Both have roots in Judaism. All 3 faiths are known as Abrahamic religions. They each recognize Abraham as their religion's first **prophet**.

THE STORY OF ABRAHAM

The story of Abraham took place over 4000 years ago. It began in the city of Ur, in Babylonia. That's in modern-day Iraq. Abraham was the son of Terach. Terach owned a shop that sold **idols** for worship. Idol worship is an example of polytheism.

THE JEWISH DIASPORA

Today, Jewish people live in countries all over the globe. This is called the Jewish Diaspora. A diaspora is the dispersion, or spread, of a people from their original homeland. The Jewish Diaspora happened over a long time. There were many events that forced Jewish people to leave. The ancient Babylonians destroyed the First Temple in Jerusalem. Jews were exiled to Babylon. Later, Romans destroyed the Second Temple in Jerusalem. The Romans tried to destroy all Jewish people. Most Jews fled. Similar events happened in different countries throughout history. The majority of Jews today live in the United States and Israel.

Yet Abraham questioned his father's religion. Over time, he came to believe that the universe was created by one God.

God and Abraham made a **covenant**. God told Abraham to leave his homeland. Abraham was to obey God in all things. In return, God would bless Abraham with a great nation. God would protect Abraham and his descendants from their enemies.

This covenant is central to Judaism. It is a contract between the Jewish people and God.

Abraham fled to Canaan with his wife Sarah. He wandered the land we now called Israel for many years. Abraham and Sarah grew quite old. Yet they had no children. Abraham took a second wife, Hagar. Hagar was Egyptian. She bore Abraham a son, Ishmael. Muslims tie their faith to Abraham through Ishmael.

At the age of 100, God promised Abraham a son to inherit the covenant. Sarah gave birth to Isaac. Both Jews and Christians tie their faith through Isaac.

THE STORY OF MOSES

Moses is the most important prophet in Judaism. His teachings can be found in the Torah, the most sacred text in Judaism. He lived roughly 400 years after Abraham. Moses is known for leading the Jewish people out of slavery in Egypt. He also delivered the Ten Commandments. These **commandments** from God are the foundation of Jewish **ethics**.

Moses was born during a time of Jewish enslavement in Egypt. It was a terrible time for the Jews. The Pharoah, or ruler of Egypt, was afraid. He was afraid the Jewish people would outnumber Egyptians. He was afraid they would want power. The Pharoah enslaved the Jewish people. But he was still afraid. He wanted to make them weak. He ordered all Hebrew infant boys to be drowned.

One woman named Yocheved wanted her son to survive. She placed Moses in a basket and sent him down the River Nile to save him. Amazingly, the basket was found by the Pharaoh's daughter. She adopted him. She was a princess. That made Moses royalty.

THE 10 COMMANDMENTS

1. Worship no god but Me.

2. Do not worship idols.

3. Do not misuse the name of God.

4. Observe the Sabbath Day (Saturday).

5. Honor and respect your parents.

6. Do not murder.

7. Do not commit adultery.

8. Do not steal.

9. Do not accuse anyone falsely. Do not lie about others.

10. Do not envy what other people have.

Moses was raised as a prince. Yet he despised the enslavement of the Jewish people. One day, God told Moses to go to the Pharaoh and tell him to free the Jews. The Pharaoh resisted. As punishment, God unleashed the Ten Plagues on Egypt. The Jewish people escaped. Moses guided them through the desert for 40 years. He led his people to the Promised Land but died before he could enter himself.

Ben
American Jew

CHAPTER 1
AN AMERICAN JEW

Ben invited his friend Liam to sleep over. Ben and Liam have been friends for years. Ben is Jewish. There are not many other Jewish kids at his school. Liam wanted to learn more. Ben invited him over for Shabbat dinner and Saturday services.

"Our **sabbath** begins on Friday evening." Ben told him. "Families gather at sundown to share a sabbath, or Shabbat, dinner." Ben's mom lights candles. She moves her hands over the flames and then covers her eyes. She says a blessing.

Next, Ben's dad says the Kiddush over grape juice. His mom has set out a Kiddush fountain. They use this when they have guests. Ben's dad pours the grape juice into the fountain. It flows out into cups set up around it. Ben offers one of the cups to Liam. Everyone in the family takes one. They all drink.

Ben shows Liam how to use the Netilat Yadayim cup to wash hands while his dad offers the next blessing.

Ben's dad then lifts the cover off the challah bread and says the last blessing. They all start to eat. Ben tells Liam that not every Jewish family has a sabbath meal each week.

"That's right," his mom says. "There are lots of ways to be Jewish. This is our way."

"We believe in God's covenant," says Ben. "God made a promise to protect all the Children of Israel. Our job is to follow God's law in the Torah. This includes the Ten Commandments. We work hard to live good lives."

The next day, Liam joins Ben at his synagogue. Liam wears a **kippah** he borrowed from Ben. Ben's synagogue asks all visitors to cover their head during services. Ben's cousin's synagogue does not do this.

The Ten Commandments are displayed in the front of the synagogue. There is a Torah ark, or special cabinet for holy text. At temple service, someone is called on to open the ark. It is an honor to be chosen. The person is told which Torah scroll to

The Jewish Bible is called the Tanakh. It has three main parts. The first part is the Torah, which contains the Five Books of Moses. The second section is called Nevi'im, which contains the books of the prophets. The third section is called Ketuvim, which includes wisdom literature like the book of Psalms.

Did you know? Jewish women traditionally lead the prayers and light the candles to begin the Jewish Sabbath.

take. They place the scroll on the rabbi's right shoulder. Then the rabbi faces the congregation and recites the Shema, a Hebrew prayer. Then he reads from the Torah.

Ben's rabbi has a **tallit** draped over his shoulders. Different people lead different parts of the service. A cantor leads the congregation in prayers and songs.

After service, Ben asks Liam what he thinks. "I didn't know so much was done in Hebrew. I knew you were learning it. I didn't realize how important it is."

Ben explains that next week will be a special service. It is his **Bar Mitzvah**. A boy becomes an adult at 13. A Bar Mitzvah celebrates his passage into manhood. "I have been learning Hebrew so I can read the Torah and other holy texts."

Did you know? A girl celebrates her passage into womanhood with a Bat Mitzvah ceremony. Some Jewish girls have a Bat Mitzvah at age 12. Others have one at age 13.

Chapter 2
A Bar Mitzvah

Ben has been practicing for his Bar Mitzvah for months. Twice a week, he visits Mr. Levi to study and practice. Mr. Levi works for the synagogue. He helps prepare all the boys Ben's age for their Bar Mitzvah. There are 3 other boys who visit Mr. Levi. But they do not go to Ben's school. They live far away. There are not many Jewish people where Ben lives and only 1 synagogue. Jewish people come from all over to attend.

Larry is leaving Mr. Levi's when Ben arrives. They stop and chat about their **haftarah**. The haftarah is a selection from one of the biblical books of the prophets. Each boy will have to recite a portion of it in Hebrew at his Bar Mitzvah.

On Saturday morning, Ben watches as the room fills up. He is wearing a tallit over his dark suit. A kippah is perched on his head. A lot of congregants from the synagogue are there. Ben's relatives sit in the front row. They have flown in from New Jersey to Tennessee to be there.

Did you know? The Torah ark is a special cabinet where the Torah scrolls are kept. Sometimes it can be fancy. It is the focal point of prayer. It is often reached by steps. The congregation stands when the Torah is removed.

When the ceremony begins, Ben helps the rabbi get the Torah scroll. He cradles it carefully. It feels heavy.

Rabbi Markovitz reads from the Torah in Hebrew. Then comes his turn. Ben begins to sweat. It is the first time he has addressed a room full of adults. He speaks quickly. Rabbi Markovitz puts his hand on Ben's arm. This is a sign to slow down. Ben takes a deep breath.

In addition to leading parts of the service and reading, or chanting, from the Torah, Ben gives a short teaching in English. His father gives him a thumbs up from the audience. Ben smiles. He did it!

Did you know? A yad is a pointer used for reading the Torah. *Yad* means "hand" in Hebrew. The Yad helps the reader follow the lines on the scroll and keep their place.

Ben is relieved when it is time for the reception. The hard part is over. Now it is time to celebrate! Everyone piles into the banquet hall at the Jewish center. There is a long table filled with food. About 20 round tables are scattered throughout the room. Ben's relatives and his parents' friends fill most of them.

Ben goes around to each table and thanks the people for coming. He shakes their hands. The adults wish him well.

"Mazel tov, Benny! Congratulations!" says Uncle Jerry. He hands Ben an envelope. "For your future. May you be blessed."

DANCING THE HORAH

The **horah** is a traditional Jewish folk dance. It is performed at weddings, and some people also do it at bat and bar mitzvah celebrations. It is usually danced to the song "Hava Nagila." The guest of honor sits in a chair. The dancers form a circle around them. The music starts slowly. So do the dancers. Then the music and dancing pick up speed. They go faster and faster. They dance with joy! They lift the chair high into the air. The guest of honor smiles and holds on. At a wedding, 2 chairs are raised up. The couple each hold onto one end of a cloth napkin. It symbolizes their union.

Esther
Israeli Jew

CHAPTER 3
AN ISRAELI JEW

Esther's stomach rumbles. This is the first Yom Kippur that she has **fasted** the full 25 hours, like an adult. She just turned 12.

Esther has not eaten since sundown the night before. Her mouth feels sticky. She does not drink water when she fasts, either. Esther's family is not very **observant**. But in Israel, many Jews fast on Yom Kippur.

The evening sun glows golden over Jerusalem. Soon, thinks Esther. Soon we'll all be together and we will eat.

Mrs. Melaku strolls by. Her white clothing flows gracefully against her dark skin. "Tsom mohil," says Mrs. Melaku.

"Tsom mohil," Esther replies. "Good fast to you."

About 75% of Israel is Jewish. The Israeli flag has two blue stripes and a Star of David. The Star of David is a popular Jewish symbol. It is named after King David, a ruler of ancient Israel.

THE HIGH HOLY HOLIDAYS

Rosh Hashanah and Yom Kippur are known as the High Holy Holidays. The 2 holidays are tightly bound together. Rosh Hashanah is the Jewish New Year. It lasts for 2 days in the fall. Rosh Hashanah celebrates God's creation of the universe. It is both a religious and celebratory time. People worship. They also gather for festive meals with symbolic food. They blow the shofar, or ram's horn. To find the new year on the Jewish calendar, add 3761 to the current year.

Yom Kippur falls 10 days later. It is the day of **atonement**. People reflect on the mistakes they have made during the year. They promise to do better. It begins before sundown and lasts until nightfall the next day. Adults neither eat nor drink for 25 hours. This includes children over 12 or 13. Dressed in white, they pray in the synagogue. The day ends when you can see 3 stars in the sky. Then the rabbi or synagogue leader blows one long blast on the shofar.

All around Esther is a sea of white linen. It is a quiet, peaceful sea. There are no cars to be seen or heard. Many people choose not to drive on Yom Kippur. There are few places to go. There is only stay. The airports are closed. So are the train stations.

Families walk in the streets as though cars and buses never existed. Children ride their bikes.

In Israel, hardly anyone works on Yom Kippur. Businesses are closed. Some people don't use their phones. Some use no electricity at all. This leaves only quiet. This leaves only the feeling of community.

Esther knows that community is important on Yom Kippur. It is a time for reflection and self-evaluation. It is a time for her to think about the things she has done. It is a time for her to think about how she can do better. Esther thinks about how she treats her friends and family. She makes a promise to herself. She will be more patient. She will offer to help more often.

At home, Esther's father offers her a snack of faloodeh. Little pieces of apple float in iced rose water. Esther is grateful for the cold treat. There are other dishes, too. There is a pot of delicious **hamin**. There is toast with melted cheese, onions, and olives. There are honey cakes and sweet pomegranates. Esther's mouth waters. The family gathers at the table. They say a prayer. Then they eat. It is the most delicious meal Esther has ever tasted. It is even more special because it is shared with the people she loves.

Did you know? Purim is a Jewish holiday with a carnival-like atmosphere. People dress in costumes. There are other fun traditions, too.

CHAPTER 4
A PURIM FESTIVAL

Esther rises before the sun. She is too excited to sleep. It is the best day of the year. Purim!

Esther greets her mother with bright eyes. "Purim sameach!" she says. "Happy Purim!"

"Chag sameach," says her mother. "Happy holiday."

The sweet smell of hamantaschen fills the house.

"Wait for them to cool," says her mother. "You and Udi can prepare your **mishloach manot** after the cookies have cooled."

Esther is eager to fill the gift boxes with delicious treats. Giving them to friends on Purim is a mitzvah, a commandment from God. So is giving to the needy.

Esther prepares her costume while she waits. Udi rolls his eyes. "Queen Esther, again?"

"You're only jealous," says Esther. "You aren't named after the hero of Purim."

"I'd rather be Spiderman," said Udi.

The first stop is synagogue. Service includes the telling of the Megillah. It is another mitzvah. The story of Esther is long. But Rabbi Mizrahi uses puppets when he tells it. Everyone shakes noisemakers when the rabbi says the wicked name *Haman*. The noise drowns out the villain's name.

Now it is time for Esther's favorite part of the day. The carnival! Safra Square is alive with color and excitement. Religious and secular groups alike fill the streets. Everyone is decked out in their best costumes. Esther and her friends weave through street

In modern times, skits or plays have become a popular way to tell the story of Megillat Esther. Puppets like these may be used.

THE MEGILLAH

The Megillah is the Book of Esther. She saved the Jews in the 5th century Persian Empire. "The whole megillah" is a popular American expression. It means "the entirety of something." It especially refers to a long story with many details.

performers and artists. They stop to play carnival games. They finish the afternoon at the parade. Jugglers, acrobats, giant puppets, circus clowns and a dizzying rainbow of costumes pass by.

The fourth mitzvah is the seudah, the Purim feast. It is a time to eat, drink, and be merry. Esther's family is having a party. Their home is filled with friends and neighbors.

Everyone sits down for the feast. Esther looks around and smiles. Everyone is still in costume. Her father gives a toast with words from the Torah. So do several other grownups. Each one

A CONTINUOUS CYCLE

There are many holidays unique to Judaism throughout the year. For example, Tu Bishvat is a day of giving. In ancient times, trees were marked. The fruit of those trees went to people in need. Today, people in Israel celebrate Tu Bishvat differently. Tu Bishvat has become an environmental awareness day. People celebrate by planting trees. Many children in the U.S. send money to Israel to plant trees. The spirit of Tu Bishvat has stayed the same. It is a day of working to make the future better for all.

Another Jewish holiday is Simchat Torah. A simcha is any happy occasion. Simchat Torah celebrates the annual cycle of Torah readings. It means "the joy of the Torah." The Torah is read throughout the year. On Simchat Torah, the cycle starts over. Public readings of the Torah go back to the beginning. The cycle begins again for the next year.

Mishloach manot set out for Purim guests

is sillier than the last. Everyone laughs and cheers. These speeches are **satire**. They are playful. Speakers pretend to be serious.

The meal goes on long past sundown. It is late when everyone goes home. Her parents have set out mishloach manot for their guests to take home. The baskets are filled with gifts of food and sometimes wine. Esther is tired but her heart sings. Another wonderful Purim has ended.

ACTIVITY

MAKING HAMANTASCHEN

Hamantaschen is a popular Purim treat. They are small triangle-shaped cookies with a sweet filling. The most popular fillings are jams. But you can use anything, like chocolate or hazelnut spread. The name refers to Haman, the villain in the Purim story.

INGREDIENTS:

3 eggs

3/4 cup oil

1/3 cup water

2 teaspoons vanilla extract

5 1/2 cups flour

1 cup sugar

3 teaspoons baking powder

filling of your choice

DIRECTIONS:

1. Preheat oven to 350°. Grease cookie sheet.
2. In a bowl, mix eggs and sugar. Stir in oil and vanilla. Combine flour and baking powder. Stir until dough forms.
3. Roll out the dough on a floured surface. Cut circles into dough using a glass rim or cookie cutter. Place circles 2 inches apart. Add a teaspoon of filling to the center of each cookie. Pinch edges to form 3 corners.
4. Bake 12–15 min. Let cool for 1 minute. Transfer to a wire rack.

TIMELINE OF MAJOR EVENTS

Circa 931 BCE: King Solomon builds the First Temple in Jerusalem.

586 BCE: The First Temple is destroyed by Babylonians.

515 BCE: Zerubbabel completes construction of the Second Temple.

473 BCE: Queen Esther helps save the Jewish people from the evil Haman.

70 CE: The Second Temple is destroyed by Romans and the Jewish people are driven out of their homeland.

1040 CE: Rabbi Solomon ben Isaac, known as Rashi, is born. His writings help transform Jewish learning.

1475 CE: The first Jewish text printed is a book of Rashi's commentary.

1492 CE: Jewish people are forced out of Spain during the Spanish Inquisition.

1654 CE: The first Jews settle in North America.

1933–1945: The German Nazi party kills 6 million Jews in the Holocaust.

1948: Israel is established as a state, creating a new home country for Jews.

LEARN MORE

FURTHER READING

Marsico, Katie. *Judaism*. Ann Arbor, MI: Cherry Lake Publishing, 2017.

Rosinsky, Natalie M. *Judaism*. Mankato, MN: Compass Point Books, 2010.

Self, David. *The Lion Encyclopedia of World Religions*. Oxford, UK: Lion Children's, 2008.

GLOSSARY

atonement (uh-TOHN-muhnt) the making of amends for doing something wrong

Bar Mitzvah (BAR MITZ-vuh) a Jewish coming-of-age ceremony for a boy

commandments (kuh-MAND-muhnts) rules from God

covenant (KUHV-uh-nuhnt) a formal agreement

ethics (ETH-iks) rules of conduct for how to behave with morals and principles

fasted (FAST-uhd) to deny food or drink

haftarah (haf-TAHR-uh) portions of the Nevi'im (the book of Prophets) read aloud during synagogue service

hamin (HA-min) a slow-cooked stew often served on the sabbath

icon (EYE-kahn) an important or holy figure used in worship

idols (EYE-dul) objects of worship that represent gods

kippah (KIP-puh) a skullcap worn by Jewish men in public or to worship

messiah (mi-SAHY-uh) the promised and expected savior of the Jewish people.

mishloach manot (mish-LOW-ach MAN-ots) baskets of food given on Purim

observant (uhb-ZUR-vuhnt) careful in following rules, laws, or customs

psalms (SAWLMZ) a book of the Bible that contains songs, hymns, and prayers

persecuted (PUR-si-kyoo-tid) regularly harassed or oppressed for one's beliefs

prophet (PROF-it) a person who speaks for God

satire (SAT-ahyuhr) a style of humor meant to poke fun at a topic

tallit (TAH-lis) a white shawl with fringes worn by Jewish men during prayer

Torah (TOH-rah) the law of God as revealed to Moses and recorded in the first five books of the Hebrew scriptures; also a scroll containing the scriptures

INDEX